P

MW00639515

"Kim takes her unspeakable heartbreak of losing a child and has turned it into comfort and healing for others when the unthinkable strikes. Kim's words in this book are a true gift to others of healing, inspiration and strength."

Lauren Finkelstein, Founder, Save 1 Person,
Author, "Save Me. Save The World: A Guide to Becoming a Superhero"

"This book is such a gift to all of us to help our closest family and friends get through the hardest days of their lives! I wish this book was around when my sister lost her daughter and my close friend lost her son. In those moments, you don't know what to do or what to say, you feel helpless. I so wanted to be there for them and what actions to take without them asking. Because honestly, they don't even know what they need! Thanks to your book I now have a tool to help and so many others will as well! Thank you!

Staci Zacher

"Kim displays passion in everything she sets her sights on. Her willingness to confront personal loss experienced earlier in life and bring direction to those enduring similar anguish is laudable. I believe her sincere and sensible guidance will provide an uncomplicated approach for families and friends confronting the daunting loss of a child."

Kim Grivner

"While no one should ever lose a child, Kim's guide can help get one through the darkest of times."

Ben Weiss, CoinFlip.tech

"Kim has brought some much-needed light on a very difficult subject. She speaks with conviction and wisdom that can only come from first-hand experience. No doubt her book will help others in their darkest times."

Chris Schafer

"At a time when there are just no words to say, many people don't know how they can help a family that just lost a child. A delicate topic that many people are apprehensive to discuss, Kim Calabrese does just that. She knows first-hand the importance of having supportive friends and family after the loss of her daughter. The invaluable insight that you will gain by reading this book will prepare you to be that vital role in someone else's life, at a time when they need you most."

Rebecca Spitz

"I found myself feeling truly relieved while reading Kim's book, because as she states, most of us are likely to find ourselves in the unfortunate, but honorary, situation of being there for someone we love when they've had a loss this great. With the knowledge and tools we get from reading this book, we can all be armed with ways to help our loved one when they are hurting the most.

In the wake of any tragedy, all we want to do is help in any way we can, and now we all know how. What a gift Kim has given the world!"

Terra Weiss

"Since I have known Kim, she has always had a big heart and a compelling drive to assist others. She has helped multiple friends cope with the loss of loved ones, especially when there was a child involved. It comes as no surprise to me that Kim would write a book to reach out to as many people as possible struggling with the death of a child, family member, or friend."

Amy Burchett

"This book can be of immense help to anyone trying to help a friend or family member who has just suffered a traumatic loss. Of course, the loss of a child is the single most terrible event in a person's life, but the loss of a close family member, or friend, can also be devastating. This book can help to guide you through the process to maximize your effectiveness in consoling the loved one and being helpful in a practical way. I have had the pleasure of knowing Kim and her family for several years, but I never realized just how strong a person she really is. In the foreword of this book, Loren Lahav mentions Kim interviewing hundreds of people who had lost a child in order to assess the proper approach at the time of such loss. I cannot imagine the strength this took, or the emotional toll it took on her, especially knowing that she had lost a child under tragic circumstances. Imagine this:

every time she spoke with a grieving parent, she had to relive her terrible loss over again. But she persevered in order to write this book to be of help to others. I am very proud to call her my friend, and my HERO."

Joseph Riotto

"I have known Kim for only a few years now. When we first met, she told me about the book she was writing and why. As a parent of three boys, I can tell you that any parents' worst nightmare is the thought of losing a child. I have thought about this so many times since the day my boys were very young and disappeared in a department store. I have often thought of what I would do and how I would handle it if lost one of my boys. I didn't know. What I did know is how angry I would be. After reading Kim's book it gave me a total roadmap of what I would have to do and why. It explained how to deal with it emotionally and logistically. Prior to reading Kim's book, I had no idea what and how I would deal with such a loss. I recommend this book to every parent that has a child and certainly ones that have lost one. The information is invaluable. Sadly, Kim knows first-hand."

Steve DeMasco, PhD
10th Degree Black Belt

"This Book is a MUST READ. Kim's personal story of the loss of her beautiful little girl serves as a roadmap for all of us...whether we suffer our own losses and or need to support a friend or family member in their time of loss. This book shows you how to create the necessary community, love, and support around the road bumps of life. It is beautifully written and amazing wisdom and insights are shared!"

Teri I. Klug

WHAT
DO I DO?

WHAT
DO I DO?

*A Step By Step guide
for **Friends and Family** to Support
Anyone Who Has Lost a Child*

KIMBERLY CALABRESE

KAT BIGGIE PRESS
Columbia, SC

What Do I Do? is published by Kat Biggie Press
http://katbiggiepress.com

Cover design by Michelle Fairbanks, Fresh Design
Interior design by Write|Publish|Sell

ISBN: 978-1-948604-44-4
Library of Congress Control Number: 2019936597

Publisher's Cataloging-In-Publication Data
(Prepared by The Donohue Group, Inc.)

Names: Calabrese, Kimberly, author.
Title: What do I do? : a step-by-step guide for friends and family to support anyone who has lost a child / Kimberly Calabrese.
Description: Columbia, SC : Kat Biggie Press, [2019]
Identifiers: ISBN 9781948604444 | ISBN 9781948604451 (ebook)
Subjects: LCSH: Consolation. | Caring. | Children--Death--Psychological aspects. | Bereavement--Psychological aspects. | Grief.
Classification: LCC BF637.C54 C35 2019 (print) | LCC BF637.C54 (ebook) | DDC 155.937--dc23

Printed in the United States of America.

First Printing: 2019

I dedicate this book to my three children.

Chance, you are an extraordinary young man,
a natural engineer and LEGO™ expert.
So proud of you son!

Blayne, you always find a way to put a smile on
everyone's face. You are smart, caring and lovable.
So proud to be your Mom!

Paris, my sweet baby girl. You are always in my heart.

"Up until now, there has been no 'guide' on how to help support someone when there is the loss of a child. Having been in that awful inner circle when my sister lost her daughter 10 years ago...it is a journey that never ends, but just evolves. I wish I had had the insight and tools that Kim has provided, so that I could have been in a better place to support my family, while also trying to cope with my own deep grief.

Thank you, Kim, for bringing your voice and personal experience to help support everyone that finds themselves thrown down this very hard road."

~Catherine Carette

TABLE OF CONTENTS

Foreword... xvii

Introduction xxiii

The Phone Call 1

The Funeral..17

How You Can Help..27

My Friend Is Hurting, What Can I Do?........................41

Siblings 51

Returning To School...67

Returning To Work..81

Support For Men..93

Future Days... 105

Appendix A: For The Grieving Parent............................ 109

Grief Resources 115

Acknowledgments... 127

About The Author 131

FOREWORD

Kim and I met at a conference during a difficult point in my life. I was stressed and anxious, and that was apparently obvious. Kim walked up to me and started talking. Somehow she could tell just by looking at me that I might need a friend, so she decided to be that person. As my friendship with Kim has grown, I've realized this is how she is in her core: kind and caring, for everyone, even strangers.

You'll feel that kindness in this book. Kim wants to help grieving families who are desperately in need of kindness, caring, and support, as they rebuild their lives after the death of a child, based on her own experience after her daughter died. Building rapport and connecting with people in need comes easily to Kim, as I experienced when we first met.

This book provides key advice and tips for you during a time when you may be worried you're going to say or do the wrong thing. Kim's words will give peace, a sense of relief, and allow you to confidently take actions to care for your loved one or friend. You'll have a clearer understanding of why even the smallest things are so important to the parents and family after a child dies.

Kim is one of the best people I can think of to write a book on how to care for a grieving family because her actions stem not only from her own experiences but from pure love for others. She always does the little things to demonstrate she cares, and that is one of her amazing qualities, and it was important to her to express that love to others who are trying to be helpful to the person in their life who needs their support. She draws people to her because she cares and will do whatever it takes to care for people—like jumping on a plane to come to see me when I needed to see a friendly face in the crowd. She cherishes the little things, and it shows up in this book.

Before writing this book, Kim interviewed hundreds of people that experienced the death of a child, and their

Foreword

friends and relatives. She spoke with people that were in different stages of grief and healing. Kim shares, from her own experience and the information she gained in all the interviews, steps and a process you can follow to help care for a friend or loved one, because a child's death, is one of the most heartbreaking times anyone will ever experience.

Kim's hope is that this book will help grieving families recover faster and live a fuller life because they were supported from the very beginning. For Kim, helping grieving parents is non-negotiable. Kim believes the world needs healing, and this is her way of doing her part. With this book, Kim has a great way to help people, give them some direction, a road map, ideas and suggestions in a time of crisis.

Loren Lahav, International Speaker,
Lifestyle & Business Coach, Author

*Your friend will never
be the same person again,
but you have the opportunity
to play a role in **who
they become.***

INTRODUCTION

*Please don't forget our child—they
will never be gone to us.*

My six-month-old daughter Paris died in 2003,
crumbling my world and changing it forever. In
a time when I desperately needed the support
of my loved ones and family, I did not know how to ask
them for the support I needed, nor did I understand the full
scope of what was to come. My support system was equally
as ill-equipped to understand what actions they might take
to help me during this chapter of my life.

What Do I Do?

I was so crushed after her death, my world fell apart. In a short period of time I lost my job, my daughter, and my husband. I was alone. Depressed. Hurting. I tried to run away from my life, thinking that would make things better for me. In hindsight, what would have really made things better for me was the support of my friends, family, co-workers, and all of the other people in my life.

Everyone's life went back to normal quickly and I was left to fend for myself. I tried to move on by jumping back into work, but that was a terrible experience and I came home every day and cried. I became so depressed and decided I had two choices; either I would commit suicide to be with my daughter, or, I was going to completely abandon my life and start new somewhere else. Thankfully, I chose option B.

At the time, my parents were off living their dream, sailing the world. This offered an opportunity for me to escape because they had a beautiful condo in Florida that was vacant, overlooking the gulf. I was able to live in this beautiful world, looking at the ocean as I drank my coffee, leaving behind my troubles and sorrows.

Life was better. Shortly before I left my old life, I met the man I am married to now, and we fell in love. He came with me to Florida, and we started our life together. I thought I had successfully run away from that painful period. I began to dream about having more children.

Happiness would not come easily for me. Tragedy struck again and I had three miscarriages over the next year. We had testing done and I was told there was nothing wrong with me physically, but I was probably too stressed, causing my body to miscarry. My husband took a job in Tulsa, Oklahoma, and we moved to a place where life was slow, calm, and I could focus on being healthy.

Finally, I became pregnant with my first son, who was also born with extreme complications and we nearly lost him. Thankfully, he survived and was healthy. Then I had a second son a couple years later. I committed myself to raising the boys, homeschooling them, and traveling. Life was good, but somewhere during this timeframe I found myself unexpectedly sucker punched with another wave of grief and depression.

That resurgence of grief made me realize that you can't hide from grief, and despite my efforts, I could not just pretend her death did not happen. When I finally stopped running from my grief and faced the depth of the depression that was impacting my life years later, I began to see how abandoned I felt after her death and how many things could have made the situation different for me.

What Do I Do?

There were many ways my friends and family could have stepped in and things they could have done for me in the aftermath of Paris's death, but I didn't know how to ask them, and they did not know what to do.

Once I came to this conclusion, I felt a need to talk to other grieving parents to find out if they'd had a similar experience. I interviewed hundreds of parents who told me they felt completely overwhelmed and alone in the months after their child died, and in hindsight, wished others had stepped in to help them with more of their day-to-day tasks or even just been there to listen to them. Many reported feeling so lost in the months after their child died, alone and isolated from the rest of the world who had moved on, struggling to make it from day to day. Some shared that it took them years to deal with the anger and grief, and wonder if they would have healed faster or better if others had shown up more for them in their time of need.

The parents aren't the only ones that suffer greatly and need help. The siblings of the child that died also shared with me how they were impacted by the loss of not only their sibling, but the parent who was no longer the mom or dad they knew before.

I know we can do better. We can make a difference in

the outcome for the families struggling to survive after such a horrific event.

What Do I Do? is my answer to this problem.

This book is to guide those who are the closest to the grieving family, providing tools and resources to help the family put their shattered lives together again. It can also be used by the grieving family as a resource to give to others when they are asked how others can help. But it can also be used by any person in your life—your hairdresser, your mailman, your child's teacher or soccer coach—anyone who has heard about your situation and wants to know how they can be helpful, can use the advice in this book.

WHAT YOU NEED TO UNDERSTAND ABOUT GRIEVING PARENTS

Before we continue, it is helpful to share some insight into what is happening in the minds of parents who've lost a child. When a child dies, the parents and the family are overwhelmed with grief, and likely in shock. Some days, it takes everything in them to even get out of bed. The first few days are filled with thoughts like, "How can I possibly go on?" and "How do I even get out of bed?". It's not uncommon for parents to report that they have few or no memories from the initial few days after the death.

Even the smallest of tasks seem daunting, and it can be exhausting to face the list of tasks that is created in the wake of their child's death. And the list of tasks is long, as I'll describe to you throughout the book. It is during the first few days and weeks that they need YOU, the friends and family, the most, to step in and take action on their behalf. In most cases, it is okay to just start doing things on their behalf. Answering the door, answering the phone, taking notes on things people offer, bring, or do. Take care of the other children, who might get lost in the shuffle, but still desperately need attention and support.

Many people are afraid to reach out or take action to help, and instead wait for the family to request help. I want people to understand that it's too overwhelming for the grieving family to try to help others learn how to help them.

If you're reading this book, it's because someone you care about deeply needs your help. I charge you, as a close friend or family member, to step up and take a lead role in coordination. Let the grieving parents decide how much or how little they want to be involved in making decisions during the days and months following the death of their child, as some will want to be really involved and others will not want to make any decisions at all.

TO THE CLOSE FRIEND, FAMILY MEMBER, OR CAREGIVER

You are the true audience of this book—the person who is going to step in and take charge of the details to allow the family some time after the death of their child. I intend for this book to guide you so that you can take actions without putting extra stress on the family. You'll learn what to expect, how to help, and the many ways in which you can offer your time and support. The book explains how you can organize and manage the efforts to help the family in the immediate aftermath and the first several months following the death of their child.

Colleagues and co-workers, teachers and school staff, and acquaintances that want to help to provide a greater sense of the situation this family is facing and what kind of support may also find this book useful. Whether the grieving parents are members of your extended family, friends, neighbors or co-workers, the entire family, including the children and the grandparents, may need an incredible amount of support.

As friends and family, you have the opportunity to help the grieving family to stay strong, take care of them, and surround them with unconditional and unwavering support. In doing so, you will relieve a tremendous burden on the family. I hope you will find this book helpful during a grieving family's time of need.

TO THE ACQUAINTANCE AND CO-WORKER

You also have an important role to play. You will interact with the grieving parent on a day-to-day basis and have the opportunity to make their life more comfortable, particularly as they return to work and daily activities. This book will give you some basic ideas on how to respond, help, and what to say.

I organized this book beginning with the immediate steps to be taken as soon as close friends or immediate family members have been notified. From there, we move into how the support team can be helpful through the different events and stages that unfold after the child dies.

TIPS IN THIS BOOK ARE PRIMARILY DIRECTED AT TWO DIFFERENT KINDS OF HELPERS:

1. The person or team that will take the lead for the family

2. Any friend who wants to share in their grief, letting the family know that they are being held close.

The worst thing you can do is nothing at all.

My biggest hope for this book is that we will be better able to support a grieving family in their worst days, and to assist in reducing their stress, anxiety, and other burdens that crop up after their child has died. Ultimately, we want to help them move toward healing in a time and manner that is comfortable and encouraging.

TO THE GRIEVING PARENT

If you are reading this book and you are the grieving parent, this is the hardest thing you have ever experienced thus far. Life is forever different. Your friends and family can play a crucial role in reducing the trauma and additional stress related to surviving the death of a child, and how your family is able to recover in the aftermath. But they may not be equipped with the skills and knowledge to do that. I wrote this book for you to give all the people in your life who ask "How can I help?" or "What Can I Do?" Don't be afraid to ask for help. People do want to help you, but usually need some direction. So this book provides the HOW.

DISCLAIMER: There are no absolutes with grief and loss.

The suggestions and tips in this book are based on my personal experience, evidence-based research articles, and most importantly, first-hand experience from the many interviews I conducted with other grieving families. I interviewed so many parents, siblings, teachers, friends, and other people impacted and I tried to pull the most common sentiments from the many interviews. But we recognize that each person grieves and heals differently. What feels good and supportive to one person may seem intrusive to another, so please take all of these as purely suggestions and try your best to apply them to your friend. If I share a tip that doesn't resonate or is uncomfortable for you, pick something that does feel right for you, and the person you are helping.

You are already showing how much you love and care for this person just by reading this book, so use the suggestions as a guide, not as an absolute. The most important thing is to step-up and do something.

With heartfelt love,
Kimberly Calabrese

"The first few weeks every-one was there to talk or listen to us. But after about two months they seemed to stop checking up on us or didn't have the energy to listen. That was what we needed most the first year."

~Helen

THE PHONE CALL

"I got the call from Kimberly, who was at the hospital with her baby, Paris. I didn't know what to do. I was frozen in fear!"
– Julie Lingenfelter, Friend

"Miss me already?" I happily answered when I saw my cousin Kimberly's name light up my phone. That greeting—one I'll never say again—is forever burned in my memory. That was a phone call I never expected, and I had no real idea of how to even process the news or how to respond. My cousin (sister, by closeness standards)

was calling to tell me that something had happened to her infant daughter and I needed to get to the hospital—now. In the first few horrific days following that phone call, my cousin lost not only her child, but also her sense of self.

Kim's transformation from a spunky, happy, loving, organized woman to a hollow body and soul was gut-wrenching to witness. My own child was due to arrive in just a couple of months and we were so excited for the future. Kim and I planned to raise our kids together. Now, that would not happen. Incomprehensibly to me, the practiced mom had lost her child while I, the unseasoned almost-mom, was preparing to bring a child into this world. I had been expecting to rely on her guidance, but suddenly it was my time to support her—in every possible way. How would I do this? No handout at the hospital instructed me how to support a mom whose world just crumbled. Even those in my network who had been in a similar situation weren't able to provide any advice beyond "Just be there for her." What does that mean? How can that ever be enough to help her in this time?

I did my best but never felt like I was really helping her. Years later, I am still amazed that she was able to pick herself up and create a beautiful life for herself and her family. We will never forget Paris, and her death has certainly shaped Kim's life into a different reality, but we are all so fortunate that "Miss Organization" is back in her saddle.

Kim has put a tremendous amount of time and effort in recalling her painful journey for this book, in order to provide context and awareness for readers. She imparts her insights and experience, spelling out ways to lift the pressure off of those at the center of a traumatic loss, but also provides useful pointers for how you can "just be there" for someone who needs a pillar of support. Kim's strong will and continued commitment to helping others is truly admirable and inspiring. When I was struggling to support Kim, I would have done anything to have a book like this to guide me through those uncertain, stressful and terrible days.

Heather Sandberg, Kim's Cousin

THE PHONE CALL AND FIRST FEW DAYS

If you're receiving one of the first phone calls from the family when a child dies, you are important to them, and needed by them immediately, even if just to be by their side and hold their hands. The "inner circle" can best help the family by relieving them of daily tasks and organizing the day-to-day care and support in the days, weeks, and even months that follow. This chapter outlines all the immediate tasks you might expect to help with as soon as you receive the phone call.

DON'T WAIT TO BE ASKED TO COME - DRIVE OR FLY

If you're part of the family's inner circle, try to get to the parents' home as quickly as possible. Don't waste time calling the parents and trying to make plans, as they will be in shock and not able to answer your questions or aid you in planning your trip. Just do what you need to do. While you may also be in shock, don't forget to tell the necessary people where you are going, check the weather for your destination, and pack appropriately. You'll want to include an outfit for the funeral and comfortable clothes for running errands and traveling.

TO DO LIST

- *Let friends and co-workers know of your absence.*

- *Check the weather for your destination, and pack appropriately. Include clothing for the funeral, as well as comfortable clothing for running errands and traveling.*

- *Pack a notebook, pens, and post-it notes.*

The Phone Call

It's useful to pack a notebook, some pens and post-it notes with your other items so that you can start helping with coordination efforts once you arrive. As the phone rings, as people arrive and offer to take care of certain tasks, as gifts are provided, you'll want to have all of this written down to keep up with or provide to the family later.

Don't stress about packing. If you forget something, you can always buy what you need once you get there. The important thing is to get to the parents as soon as possible.

I got the call from Kimberly, who was at the hospital with her baby, Paris. I was in bed and had no clue what to do. Frozen in fear, I remember I actually asked HER what I should do. She responded calmly, "You need to come to the hospital." And I did so calmly, only because that's the example she set. As I flash back to the hospital, I remember my best friend speaking so serenely when she informed us that Paris was brain dead and the best thing to do was to take her off life support. Who can do this? She is the strongest woman I know!

That night, after Paris died, I remember lying in bed with Kim and Heather, another dear friend. While Kim was being our source of support, as she has always been, we were falling apart. Kim stayed strong and in charge. I remember her telling US what to do! I remember being with Kim and by her side no matter what, but Kim was directing us the entire time—we got through it because of her! She is amazing! Seventeen years and many trials, losses, and heartaches later, my best friend is helping people again, just as she always has. She may not realize that what she does with ease and grace is perhaps her life's purpose. I am blessed to call her my friend!

Julie Lingenfelter, Friend

If the child is an older child, you'll likely have many people flocking to the house immediately when they receive the news. One of the stories of an older child's death that stuck out to me was shared by Amy. Amy's daughter was the close friend of a high school student that died. Her perspective is that of a friend who responded to the family after their son died.

Amy's daughter was close friends with a boy that died unexpectedly their senior year of high school in a car crash. Amy and the other parents went immediately to the house when they learned the news of the car crash. Amy set to work answering the door, answering the phone, taking notes to have available for the parents later, and running errands. She shared that she took care of tasks like getting the jacket dry cleaned they wanted him to be buried in, picking up the mother's medicines from the pharmacy, and keeping the kitchen clean. She cleaned out the refrigerator to ensure there was space for all of the food that was coming, and kept herself busy doing anything around the house she could do to make life easier for the parents. Since the child was older, there was a steady stream of friends (both his and of the parents) who came to pay their respects.

The list of tasks that follow the death of a child is long. Most parents will be in a complete state of shock and may find it difficult to complete even the simplest of tasks. It is helpful if one or two people closest to the family take the lead in organizing the planning efforts, especially those things that need to be handled immediately. Do not wait for the family to ask you to help, because they probably aren't even aware of what help they need, or are too exhausted to try to help you help them. The following few sections are tips to help with organization and planning of support.

ORGANIZING FAMILY AND GUESTS

When you arrive, you may be the first person, or there may already be other people gathering. Greet the grieving parents and their other children, then assess the situation to determine what has already been done and what still needs to be organized. The first few days, your major role is to handle logistics and other people, so that the family is not overwhelmed. Be gentle with the family, as they might not have the capacity to make decisions or have the energy to engage in long conversations. On the other hand, some parents may throw themselves into doing the things that they feel compelled to take care of personally, or as a way to distract themselves from the crushing grief. Observe and determine the action steps that are best suited for you to take on based on their response and what will help ease their burden the most.

ACTION STEPS:

1. Help with notification efforts. Make a list of people who need to be called:

   - *Friends*

   - *Family*

   - *Co-workers*

   - *Neighbors*

2. Make the phone calls on behalf of the family, if that is their preference. Or send emails.

3. Coordinate any logistical information for people traveling in for the funeral.

   - *How are family and guests arriving? Are they driving in? Flying in? Do they live locally?*

   - *Create a "who's who" list in your notebook and start writing things down.*

   - *For friends and family members will be traveling to attend services or to help the family, be sure to include who is arriving, their date and arrival times, and travel arrangements. When you talk to them, let them know you will be providing details about the funeral arrangements in the next few days, in order to stem the onslaught of calls to the grieving family, in search of information. Determine who can help with picking up people from the airport. Perhaps a neighbor or friend of the family can help you or you can provide them with a taxi, Uber, or Lyft details, or even volunteer a car to be borrowed. Every resource helps.*

4. Don't forget the children! Taking care of the other children is a priority task. Make sure there is someone dedicated to caring for the other children so they are

not forgotten in the shuffle. Please see the chapter "Siblings" for details on how to talk to the children and help care for them.

5. Take care of errands that need to happen for the family or around the house.

ACCOMMODATIONS

Where will incoming family and guests be staying? At the family's home, (with the family's permission) at a hotel, or with friends nearby? You can do a Google search for local hotels, Airbnbs, or extended stay residences nearby. Most hotels will give a special rate for funeral guests and family members. Compile a list, and email it to the arriving family and guests.

FOOD AND REFRESHMENTS

You will want to consider food for family and friends who are coming into town, for the funeral and any type of reception hosted, and for long-term care of the family. It may be several weeks or months before the family is ready to be fully back on their feet again. One of the biggest impacts of grief is that it makes even small tasks like grocery shopping and cooking a meal seem incredibly overwhelming.

You'll want food available at the house for family and visitors. There is a high probability that friends and neighbors will start bringing food, meals, snacks, and so forth. If you need more you can pick things up at the market, Costco, order food for delivery from nearby stores or ask a family member or friend to bring something—drinks, snacks, frozen meals or casseroles. Paper plates, glasses, and plastic silverware can also be a big help to keep the kitchen tidy.

It's helpful to provide sandwiches, snacks, and drinks to visitors and the family. Other ideas of simple items to have on hand are fruit plates and vegetable platters. Remember that many people will bring food when they visit, so don't feel compelled to overstock the fridge. Assign someone to manage the food—this way you can stay with the family and be there to help with anything that comes up.

FUNERAL ARRANGEMENTS

A difficult, but critical, part of helping is assisting the big decisions to be made immediately following the death. An important topic to discuss with the parents concerns the funeral arrangements. Ask them their preferences on location and if they want help with this intimate task. They may or may not want someone else to take on this task, but you should bring the topic up, because even if they would prefer for someone else to handle the details, the grieving parents may not want to burden anyone with this task.

Funeral arrangements can be an overwhelming process. If they would like outside help with this task, here are some questions to consider:

- *Do they have a funeral home in mind?*

- *Will there be an obituary and who will write it?*

- *Is there a family plot or funeral services already in place for the family?*

- *Are they considering cremation?*

- *Are they going to use a church, chapel or other location for the service?*

- *Which clergy, if any, needs to be notified?*

- *Is there a group at their place of worship that will assist in preparing for the service?*

- *Are there are any music selections or religious passages that they'd like?*

- *Will there be a reception or life celebration after the funeral?*

- *Do they know whether they want flowers or donations?*

The Phone Call

This is a conversation during which you'll want to take a lot of notes. The answers to these questions are important and the parents may not remember much of the conversation. If you'd prefer, you may ask the family if you can record the conversation so that there is a record of what they decide. Volunteer to make the phone calls to arrange an appointment with the funeral home. If they would like the support, go with the parents to that appointment and take notes.

Once there is a plan in place for the funeral, start reaching out to put a team together to carry it all out. When it comes to the details like organizing the food, managing the reception, and any of the other less personal details, try to reach out to people who are not immediate family members to reduce a little of the burden on yourself and other immediate family members and close friends.

WHAT TO OFFER

I recommend talking to close friends about giving money to help with the daily tasks that the family will need instead of sending flowers. Often there are an overwhelming amount of flowers, which are beautiful, but not as helpful as financial support, gift cards, or other ways to support the needs of the family. After the death of a child, services such as a house cleaner, child care, lawn care, pet supplies, groceries, or prescriptions, can be very helpful as well as cash to cover funeral expenses and any medical bills, to name a few examples.

THE GRANDPARENTS ARE MOURNING TOO

If you are working hard to help the parents on your own and without a support team, consider not placing the burden on the grandparents. Remember the grandparents are grieving the death of their grandchild and for their suffering child, because they cannot fix this for their child. Therefore, if you need others to help with activities, reach out to other friends and family before the grandparents, unless the grandparents ask to be included.

This should give a good idea of tasks, although there may be many other things to consider. Pull together the team and assign tasks based on who is available and able to do each one.

"As soon as we learned Rachel's schoolmate had been killed, we went to their house. I set to work answering the phone, and taking messages, running errands. These were things the parents did not need to worry about." ~ friend of a family that lost a teenage son.

THE FUNERAL

Gently, friends may ease your pain.

I heard one sentiment over and over in the many interviews conducted about the day of the funeral—do not leave us alone at the funeral. Parents and siblings need someone by their side at the viewing, the funeral, any type of service, and the reception. This time is so overwhelming, the best thing you can do is provide support, love, and protection for them. You want to avoid forcing them to make decisions or do things they aren't ready to do, and help them by taking actions on their behalf on things they don't really need to be dealing with to ease their burden.

You also should be paying attention to their well-being knowing and if they look like they are exhausted, give them a break from other people. The funeral is going to be emotionally and physically draining as they go through the motions and actions surrounding burying their child, and they need you to help.

While you're helping mom and dad, don't forget the other children as well. It's equally as important to have someone with the children at all times so that they are not overlooked or forgotten about during this very confusing and sad time.

WHAT CAN I SAY?

Knowing what to say is one of the hardest parts of trying to console a grieving family at the funeral. Remember that there is nothing you can do to make it better. Some people fear saying the child's name, as if it will bring more hurt and pain, but this is generally not the case. Keep your words simple.

You might be worried about what you are going to say to them, but the parents are also nervous about what you might be about to say.

You don't have to say anything at all. Just being there is often enough. But if you feel that you must say something, here are some things you can say:

- *I'm sorry for your loss.*

- *I love you.*

- *I'm here to listen whenever you need me.*

- *You and _____are in my thoughts and prayers.*

- *I'm not sure what to say—just know that I am here for you.*

Sometimes in life we just need a hug—no words, no advice, just a hug, to make us feel like we matter.

Some of the most harmful things are said when people blurt out what they thought was a helpful statement. A simple, "I'm here for you," or "I love you," or just the silent hug is enough.

Listening, if they want to be heard, is often the best gift you can give.

As much as you might feel inclined to give it, a grieving parent does not want to receive advice or hear that it's all for the best. Even making statements like, "it will be okay one day", especially on this day, can be hurtful.

I do not want to emphasize the things you shouldn't say, because I want your focus to be on what you should do. But many people report being hurt by things people said in a moment of discomfort and it's worth taking a moment to provide some examples of harmful statements.

What Do I Do?

When a child dies, we tend to want to fix the problem and most of us can put ourselves in that situation and feel their pain. When we start to say I'm sorry and we see the person cry, we continue to talk and we start to say things that we shouldn't say, such as, "Your child is in a better place." Although you may walk away not remembering what was said, the parents do, and it hurts.

Avoid phrases like:

- *Everything happens for a reason*

- *You still have your other children*

- *You can have another baby*

- *It's all part of God's plan*

- *They're in a better place now*

Even if these are things you truly believe, these are not helpful statements.

This is just a short list to provide an idea of the things that might prove more harmful than helpful. There are no words to fix the grieving parents, so quiet comfort is better than advice or words you may later regret. In this moment it's important to understand that you cannot fix them because they are completely broken. But you can be there for them.

WHAT TO DO FIRST (FOR THE COORDINATOR/KEY HELPERS)

During the viewing at the funeral as well as at the luncheon or reception following the funeral, you'll want to make sure that someone is with the parents at all times. Keep an eye on them to see if they need something, be there to field questions, take notes when people volunteer help, and watch for signs that the family may be overwhelmed. (They may need breaks from time to time to be alone, or just with the spouse or children.)

No parent is prepared to go through what they're going to experience the next three to four days of their lives, and it's comforting to have another person there to answer questions, direct other people, or simply hold their hand. This duty might be shared by a couple of people, because you'll need breaks too. You can plan to take shifts so that someone is always available for the parents.

During the reception, watch the family to see if they may be in need of a break. It's okay to pull them away from the reception line if they look overwhelmed.

WHAT TO DO AT THE FUNERAL AND RECEPTION

Direct other people, answer questions, and gather information. You can coordinate the many requests to help. Remember to bring a notebook and pen. Many people will want to know what the parents need or what they can do to help. The parents aren't going to have any idea, nor will they care too much about these details, but you can collect contact information, and reach out to these people once you have a specific ask for them. Be sure to write down their name, email address, phone number, how they know the family, and what they are offering to do to help.

When friends or family finish speaking with the parents, you can ask them if they'd be willing to make a meal for the family or help with other activities around the house. Collect their contact information and let them know you'll contact them with more details or a link to sign up to provide a meal. Be sure to follow up and be willing to make phone calls to ensure the slots are filled.

There are many great organizations that provide this service - TakeThemAMeal.com, mealtrain.com, giveinkind. com, and others. You will probably be too busy to take everyone's information down. Either provide a sign up sheet that asks for name, email address, phone number and relationship to the parents, or assign the task of collection to someone else-- there will always be someone who wants to be useful and will be honored to be given a task.

OUT OF TOWN FRIENDS & FAMILY

People from out of town will also want to help.

Here are some ideas:

- *Gift cards for local restaurants, based on the family's preferences*

- *Gift cards for DoorDash or a similar service, if available in their area*

- *InstaCart or Prime Now gift cards, if available in their area*

- *Meal prep kit subscriptions such as Blue Apron and Hello Fresh*

If out of towners offer to have a meal delivered, assign them a specific day and be sure to follow up. If you are using a sign-up service such as SignUpGenius or one of the previously mentioned sites (MealTrain.com, etc), many *allow for the option of gift cards or give local suggestions based on the family's input for delivery. (You can also set up these websites to allow for people to sign up for helping in other ways - coming in to clean the house, picking up the other children for a playdate, running errands, yard work, etc.)* Just be sure you follow up and keep track. You don't want them having a meal delivered on the same day someone local is making one.

Using an online system such as MealTrain.com, TakeThemAMeal, GiveInKind, or Sign Up Genius will lessen the burden of keeping track of the many people who want to help. If you choose not to use an online service, know how to organize your list. Be warned, this can get very overwhelming and difficult to manage. A spreadsheet will be useful. The tools described above really do simplify the process. Regardless of the system you use, it will take careful planning and consistency to make this run as smooth as possible but the burden you are taking off the parents by coordinating this is a tremendous help.

"What I needed most from others was to be there if even it was just silence. I also needed the push, the permission to feel OR to be numb. I needed people to show up for me."
~Jackie

HOW YOU CAN HELP

Losing a child is like losing your soul.

O nce the funeral is over, you and hopefully your team of helpers, can truly make a difference in their healing and recovery process by taking over or assisting with the many day-to-day activities for the home and family.

You are going to want to put together a group of people that you can call on for help. As much as you want to do it all, you can't. Find out who is willing to do what, and assign tasks.

TASKS AT HOME

There are many basic tasks you can take on without even asking the parents. Food has to be made, the kitchen has to be cleaned, the pets have to be fed, the yard needs to be mowed, the housework still has to happen. Try to do as many of those types of things as you can. Then ask the parents about other things that they may need help with—like picking up prescriptions or drycleaning, paying bills, or taking the car to get the oil changed. Is there anything that needs to be taken care of for the other children? How can you be most of help to them and reduce the stress of their daily burdens?

MAKE A LIST

There are so many opportunities to help. Friends and family can show support and reduce a large burden for the family by handling necessary daily chores and duties. Remember, every family is different, so be sure to confirm any help they may need.

Make a list of the family's daily activities including laundry, doing the dishes, making lunches, grocery shopping, running errands, taking children to their usual activities, caring for pets, and so forth.

How You Can Help

In the first couple of days, it's worth looking around the house to get an idea of what their needs may be until they are able to identify their needs. Check the house and make sure they have the basics like laundry detergent, dish soap and toilet paper, and food staples such as milk, bread, eggs, and anything the kids need.

Consider seasonal needs. In winter, will they need snow removal? Lawn care if it is summer? Do they have someone they use already? Do they need help financially? (The answer to this question is almost always YES. A funeral can be quite expensive. If the child was ill, they likely have medical expenses, etc.)

If there are other children in the family, you'll want to try to get the kids back into their normal routine as quickly as possible and assist with getting them to school and activities. Will the surviving child(dren) need rides to their usual activities? Will they need lunch made? You'll find more information about how to help the children in the chapter on siblings.

Although seemingly insignificant, grocery shopping can be the hardest chore. Making even basic decisions can be difficult when you're in the worst stage of grief, and trying to plan out meals and grocery lists is a big task. Additionally, children and babies are often in stores with their parents and that reminder can be really painful.

One thing that may get overlooked is thank you cards. You can help them with thank-you cards to everyone who attended the funeral, made, or bought meals, if this is something that feels like a priority. You can pre-write some cards so that the parents only need to sign their name while you address the envelopes and place them in the mail.

Finally, don't underestimate the power of just being there. Especially if one of the parents has to return to work before the other, or children return to activities, and out of town guests go home, being alone after the funeral can be difficult. This is an important question to ask the parent—how they feel about being alone. Some people would rather be alone, and others are terrified of it.

FOOD

By this point, you'll probably have a lot of food on hand, and people scheduled to bring meals but if not, you may want to get some basic groceries. Be sure to get the items that are familiar to the children. Ask them what their favorite cereal and snack foods are, if you don't already know.

Keep an eye on the signup sheet and follow up with the out of towners who volunteered to help. Make sure there are meals planned for a couple of months.

OTHER TYPES OF HELP

Support Groups

Nothing replaces the comfort of close friends and family. While there are support groups available, many people are not ready to go talk to strangers at the beginning or are not able to take on listening to other people's stories while they are trying to handle their own pain. You, the close friend, the family member, the neighbor, the hairdresser, have the opportunity to provide a wonderful level of support for them by listening, allowing them to shed their tears, talk about their child, or vent their anger, frustrations, or fears.

You can also do some research on their behalf and gently suggest a support group for them, if you think they are the type that would prefer that. Some grieving parents really appreciate being in a room of people who "get it" while others need the time to heal more before they are with other grieving parents.

There are online support groups as well as groups you can physically go to, and if they are interested, tell them you'd be happy to look into it. Tell them you would also accompany them if it made them more comfortable.

There are family support groups, husband and wife support groups, as well as individual support groups, even some focused on siblings and children. National Alliance for

Grieving Children and Compassionate Friends are options, as well as many local grief support groups through churches and hospitals. If they are absolutely uninterested, gently suggest it once a month because their minds may change as time continues.

However, some parents will never want to attend local support groups, but might be interested in looking at websites, reading books, or finding other resources. If your friend continues to reject your suggestion of attending a local support group, do not push them, and perhaps don't offer it more than a couple of months, or you may anger them. Be there for them, listen to them, and share other resources. (We've provided pages of resources for the grieving parents at the end of the book, but again, this should be IN ADDITION TO your time and support, not in replacement of you.)

When Life Returns to "Normal" for everyone else

We expect families to return to normal very quickly, but the first year to two years is still very painful, especially since everyone around them moves on with their normal routine. Everyone grieves differently, but the first year is intense and they will continue to need you.

It is highly unlikely that the parents are "fine" within the first year or two, even if they appear to have returned to normal or tell you that they are okay. Continue checking in on them and remembering the child they lost. It is okay to talk about the child, to remember that child existed. Talking about the child is far better than pretending nothing happened.

For the first year, many grieving parents remember everything for every single day of the year and are triggered easily by memories, special days or events, their child's firsts, etc. Many grieving parents refer to the first year as though they were in a huge fog. You may have to ask them if they need to go to the store or if they are forgetting anything important that needs to get done. Reach out and take charge—you just have to ask. It is a matter of communicating with them every week and staying consistent over the first few months especially.

Always remind them it is okay to forget things, it is okay to feel emotions, it is okay to ask favors and let others help out around the house and with miscellaneous tasks, and that it is okay to lean on others through the grieving process.

For the rest of their lives, the family will feel this loss. It's not abnormal for parents to commemorate the anniversary of the death for years afterward. One family reported hosting a celebration each year on the anniversary of the child's death, for several years, gathering the friends and sharing special memories. Others may commemorate with some type of ceremony or activity. This is a coping and healing mechanism, and it's important that you support these events, even if you don't understand.

Holidays

Holidays are often trigger events and can cause significant grief. Quite simply, the holidays suck for grieving families.

Reach out to the grieving parents on and around holidays, birthdays, significant anniversaries and special days. But try not to ask excitedly about Christmas, the Holidays, or other breaks because while yours may have been fantastic, it's likely theirs was terrible.

Don't forget Mother's Day and Father's Day - even (or especially!) if the child who passed was an only child. They are still parents and will be especially sad on those days in which they will be overwhelmed with family pictures and other sad reminders.

TANGIBLE WAYS TO SHOW YOU'RE THINKING OF THEM

- *Send a card*
- *Make a donation in their memory*

- *Give an ornament with the child's name*

- *Give small tokens periodically to cheer up the family*

- *Perform a random act of kindness or participating in an awareness event in memory of the child*

- *Organize a memorial event or celebration on the one year anniversary - a butterfly release or something else to show the family you still care and remember.*

If these suggestions do not feel comfortable, there are countless ways you can make a big difference for your loved one's family while they are grieving. Most importantly, don't forget that while the rest of the world is moving on, their lives are still shattered. And it will take a long time to pick up the pieces.

Today I wrote a note to a bereaved mother. I wanted to say don't believe all those sympathy cards. The ones that say "time heals" and "God only takes the best" and "may your sorrows be lessened." You'll only be disappointed. I wanted to say this is the most heart-wrenching, chest crushing, breath stealing tragedy on earth. I wanted to tell her there will be days she wants to die, and friends who will not understand some of the things she does or says.

I wanted to tell her she will still feel her child's presence at times, sometimes so strongly that it is as if they are dancing just at the edge of whatever activity is going on. And other times she might not feel their presence at all.

I wanted to tell her that her life will not go back, that she will never be the same, because a piece of her left with her child. And that even though the pain does not go away, somehow her soul will eventually make enough room so she can hold it all– the grief, the pain, the joy and the love.

I wanted to tell her... but I didn't. Instead, I wrote this: I'm sending love, for words are pointless right now. And that is the truth.

Susi Costello

*We are unsure of which pain
is worse,
the shock of what happened or
that we will never get to
experience anything
ever again with our child.*

MY FRIEND IS HURTING, WHAT CAN I DO?

*If you put yourself in uncomfortable
situations to help friends, you will
become an expert at helping others.*

We live in a busy world, moving quickly from one thing to the next. But when someone's child dies, their world comes to a complete and jolting halt. You are their friend, their family member, their support system. You will be needed, and for a long time. As bystanders, we often try to impose our own timeline and our own beliefs on how others should handle their

41

grief and loss, and it can be very challenging to understand what they are experiencing, especially if you've never been through this. But you are so desperately needed, even if you think you are not.

It's not always easy to show up for your friend. It's not always convenient. And sometimes they are not going to be easy to be around. Depending on your situation, it may also be difficult for the grieving parents to be around you.

MY COUSIN'S STORY

My cousin and I grew up like sisters—we couldn't have been closer. Neither of us ever wanted children growing up, but I eventually ended up getting pregnant. I was excited about the pregnancy, so then my cousin decided wanted a child of her own too.

We wanted to raise them together, close like we were. My cousin was seven months into her pregnancy when Paris died. The news hit her hard but did her best not to say or do things that might hurt me. As you might imagine, she was unsure how to behave around me without saying or doing things that would trigger my pain. How could she celebrate her pregnancy when she knew I was suffering so much from the death of my own daughter? She didn't want to cause me pain.

When her son was born, she questioned whether she'd be able to bring him around me without causing intense pain.

It was hard for both of us because I could no longer be there for her, either—I was supposed to be planning her baby shower, but I couldn't help anymore, nor did I attend.

It was a huge tragedy for both of us when Paris died. Looking back, she has shared with me if she'd had a book like this, there are many things she would have done differently to support me more. She could have done many things from afar: sent meals, called me or texted me to check in, or made sure someone else was tasked to keep tabs on me.

SUPPORTING YOUR FRIEND

Your friend needs your support to survive day-to-day life in the weeks and perhaps even months following the death of their child. Social anxiety after losing a child is a very common event. Even going to the grocery store or out to run errands can provoke anxiety in the mother or father that people are talking about them, avoiding them, or feeling pity. It is not uncommon for people to shy away from saying anything at all. The lack of acknowledgment about the child's death is even worse than saying the wrong thing.

What Do I Do?

Your friend has just experienced a significant and deep traumatic event. In addition to anxiety, they may actually be re-traumatized by places, smells, sounds. Some parents will suffer from Post Traumatic Stres Disorder (PTSD) and as a close friend, it's your job to pay attention to signs that they may be struggling.

The first year will be challenging because your life will continue on and go back to normal. Life will become busy again, and you may find it hard to understand what is happening with your friend. You might find that you try to check in with them or invite them places and they decline. Sometimes it is easier to be alone than it is to be in public, avoiding awkward conversations and glances. Try to put yourself in their shoes—they may not necessarily want to be alone, but it may be too difficult to go out. Continue to check in with your friend, visit them as they feel comfortable with, and invite them out. They may decline many of your invitations, for various reasons, but continue to invite the parents. Don't give up on them, they'll be ready again eventually to resume social activities. Show them you care, are thinking of them, and still want them actively in your life.

Expect that they will not attend anything focused on or around children—birthdays, baby showers, baptisms, and other events that can be very painful. Accept this as part of the grieving process. The grieving parents will appreciate every invite, though it may be challenging for you to understand why they may refrain from attending such events. Their grief is still too raw, they are suffering too much, and they may be afraid that their emotions will take over, stealing the limelight from a person's special day.

It can be so comforting to have a weekly plan to spend time with him/her, with your friend's permission and constructed based on his/her level of comfort in those first few months. If you're able to, establish a routine for the same time each week so that it is something he/she will look forward to. During these visits, you can offer to take your friend out for a while—a walk, out to lunch, or to get coffee. Try to avoid places where there may be a lot of children as this can be sensitive and painful. Your friend may not want to leave the house and that's ok, but still show up just to listen. Give your friend permission to talk about their child, and if they want to, they will share openly about what is going on. Parents often want to tell the story over and over again to make some sense of what has happened and also to remember their child.

Listening allows for important healing during the grieving process. If the grieving parents ask you a question, they may not really want an answer, they may just need you to listen to their thoughts. If there is an awkward silence, just say, "I'm so honored to be here and listen" to offer permission to keep talking. They might tell you the same story a hundred times. Be patient.

In the first few weeks, daily phone calls are extremely important so they do not feel forgotten. Your friend may not answer every day, depending on how they feel. Some people do not want to talk, even to their closest friends, on bad days. Some couples need some time to process on their own as well. If a couple of days pass without your friend answering any calls, see if they'll respond to texts. Texting from time to time is ok but remember, hearing your voice even if left in a message, is crucial.

The only way to know if your friend is functioning and getting out of bed is to check on them periodically. If you notice they are not getting out of bed or handling day-to-day activities, after weeks and months, they may need to get to see a doctor to help them get through this tough time.

If there are siblings and the parents are not functioning, friends and family will need to step in and make sure the children's needs are being met. Don't let the children get lost along the way. You might help them find support groups and counseling, which are not only a good idea in the first year or two after the child dies, but also during any major life and family changes that may trigger grief.

Hopefully, there will be days you see them smile and while that is an important step during grief recovery, don't assume they have healed. Instead, try to recall what you said or did that made them smile and provide opportunities to provide them with moments of joy. Laughter and smiling are wonderful gifts you can give to your friend.

Each person will grieve differently and their timeline will be different. A large part of grief is processing and everyone processes differently, and at different rates. Some need constant companionship, others need quiet space. You are providing a great gift and impacting how they heal by being there for them in a nonjudgmental and supportive manner.

MOVING ON AFTER LOSS

At some point, your friend may ask you what you think about them having another baby.

In this case, return the question to them. Ask them if they feel ready to have another baby.

If you have not experienced this loss yourself, refer them to parents who have gone through this, whether a support group or online resource, such as Still Standing or Pregnancy After Loss Support. If your friend does decide to have another baby, don't think this is going to solve all of their problems. Being pregnant after loss is a very emotional process. They might be very excited at the beginning but the emotions will roll in.

I remember when I found out I was having a boy after my daughter died. I was devastated. The thought of having a boy never crossed my mind. I truly believed I would have a girl to fill the void from the baby girl I was missing so desperately. It was yet another emotional hurdle that I had to come to terms with. Additionally, there are often fears throughout the pregnancy that something bad will happen to this baby, and then when the baby is born, emotions and postpartum hormones kick in ferociously. This can bring back many memories triggering grief, including the birth of the now deceased child. Although it is typical for parents to do their best not to compare the new baby to the deceased child, it sometimes happens anyway.

"My husband had to go out of town the week after the funeral. My best friend stayed every night that he was gone with he was gone just so I wouldn't feel so alone."
~ *Tammi M.*

SIBLINGS

If your friend is not the same friend they
once were, they are also not the same parent.

Just like adults, children grieve in their own manner and own timeline. The severity of their grief and their response is based heavily on their age and stage of development when their sibling dies, and it's hard to predict. Children like routine and need a feeling of safety, security, and a sense that everything is going to be okay. As a friend, you can try to help keep the children's routine as normal as possible.

DON'T FORGET THE OTHER CHILDREN

"MY PARENTS ARE NO LONGER
THE SAME PARENTS."

The death of a sibling will throw the entire family's life into chaos. All of a sudden the siblings' routine may be thrown off track. Other people may be taking them to and from school, keeping them overnight, or watching them while their parents attend to the details. Younger children especially function better under routine, and this disruption can cause them to act out.

Meanwhile, their loving parents are sad and acting differently. Add in a funeral, the commotion associated with extra visitors and activities, and you have a very stressful environment for the children. The emotional needs of the children cannot be overlooked while planning out all the details and caring for the parents. Be sure that the siblings are not left alone to deal with their own loss. While counselors and grief experts do not recommend shielding the emotions from children, keep in mind that the intensity of the emotions around them may be scary. Distractions can be a good idea.

Psychologists are in agreement about several key things when it comes to talking with children about death. Children are curious and will have questions, but can easily be confused by word choice, so it's best to provide truthful answers. There are many fabulous resources to help parents and caregivers respond and care for the other children, some of which are listed at the end of this chapter, and more are provided in the chapter on siblings.

Don't under estimate the role that activities like art, music, and creation can play for children. These can be really effective with helping children heal and express their emotions.

Some common tips shared by experts include:

Do:

- *Tell the truth, but gauge how much the child can handle and perhaps give the information in small doses*

- *Cry together and share your emotions*

- *Admit if you don't know the answer to something*

- *Allow the child to participate in the services and prepare them for what may happen.*

- *Explore and identify ways the child can still feel connected to their sibling*

- *Show them it is always okay to talk about their sibling, even if it makes them sad*

Don't:

- *Be afraid to talk to the child about the person who died and allow them the space to ask their questions and feel their emotions.*

- *Hide your tears or sadness.*

- *Try to define the way that they grieve - each child responds differently.*

- *Stop them from laughing and having fun.*

Common responses by children to the death of a sibling:

- *Fears and anxiety, including nightmares and fear of abandonment.*

- *Feeling as though they have been forgotten while the family focuses on the deceased child.*

- *Some children may mimic the symptoms of their sibling.*

- *Guilt*

- *Regression to how they were in a time that was safer - if they are potty trained, they may begin to have accidents again, may wake up in the night, etc.*

CARING FOR THE OTHER CHILDREN

Caring for the other children in the home has to be one of the first and top priority assignments. In the days immediately following the death of their sibling and during the funeral, ensure someone is with the children at all times who can keep an eye on them and listen to their questions or concerns. We don't want the children to get lost in the shuffle while everyone is busy taking care of tasks and may assume the kids are okay when they aren't. This is a confusing time for them, and they need guidance, and reassurance.

Younger children will have a lot of questions, as they do about everything. They may experience similar emotions to their parents, depending on their age—disbelief, anger, sadness, or just a complete lack of understanding about where their brother or sister has gone. It is helpful to have someone talk with those children who can offer an age-appropriate explanation of what death means. If this person is you, you may want to start by asking them what their understanding of death is, gauge their thoughts and emotions. You can ask the child to share what they think death means. When talking to them, let them know that their mommy and daddy are very sad, and that they are going to see them cry and that it is okay. Reiterate that it's okay for them to cry and be sad, but it's also okay to carry on and play. It's not a bad thing that they want to carry on, but they often need that verbal permission.

At night, you might want to consider having someone sleep in their room with them, or at least stay with them until they fall asleep, because they may be terrified to go to their bedroom alone at night. Sometimes, it might be better for the siblings to stay with close relatives or a friend during this time but this should be up to the child and the parents. They might not want to leave their house, but someone needs to stay with them. They should not be left alone dealing with their own unanswered questions and pain. Be sure there is someone with them to help them understand what is going on.

It is also helpful to arrange playdates as much as possible. This will give the parents time to grieve without distractions, and allow the children to be in a positive environment where they can be kids and laugh and play. Sometimes it is hard for kids to be kids when they see their parents so sad.

THE IMPACT OF TRAUMA

Trauma impacts children differently than adults, and studies have shown that, depending on the life-stage in which the event occurs, bereavement can have significant long-term impacts on medical, psychiatric health, and behavior of children.[1]

It is not encouraged to impose adult-like responses to grief on children because of the confusion that can occur when they are forced to respond to something that they do not understand or in a way that is difficult for them. It is common for a young child to announce to everyone they see that their "baby sister died" as a way to determine how that information is received and responded to. The intense emotional response can be scary to children, and children under the age of four cannot really even comprehend mourning.

The child's reaction to the death will vary based on their age and development and should be monitored to make sure their response is within normal expectations. However, if the child continues to act out, have issues, cause disturbances,

---

1 Institute of Medicine (US) Committee for the Study of Health Consequences of the Stress of Bereavement; Osterweis M, Solomon F, Green M, editors. Washington (DC): National Academies Press (US); 1984. (https://www.ncbi.nlm.nih.gov/books/NBK217849/)

wet the bed, and do other things that are out of the ordinary, it may be time to consider taking the child to a doctor. The impact of unresolved grief or even issues that stem from being in a family where mom and dad have emotionally or mentally checked out can have a long-lasting impact on their mental health. As a close friend or family member, it may be up to you to pay attention to any warning signs that the child is not coping well.

Keeping children's lives as normal as possible and making sure they still feel loved and secure is a big part of helping them cope and maintain good mental health. Thankfully there are a growing number of resources to help children who are grieving. The National Alliance for Grieving Children is a fantastic place to start if you're looking for information and resources.

You can find local support groups, activity books and more on the website https://childrengrieve.org/.

HOLIDAYS AND SPECIAL EVENTS MUST CONTINUE

Surviving the death of a child can consume parents' attention, taking up any energy they have, with none left to give to their other living children. Holidays, events, traditions, annual trips, and so forth might seem too painful or overwhelming for the parents to plan or participate in. Sometimes, especially in the first year, the parents may cancel or opt out of participating in the usual activities because they are too distracted, too numb, or simply too overwhelmed to take on the responsibility of planning events and getting caught up in celebrations that will not include their deceased child. This can be really upsetting to the siblings, especially during the holidays.

During my interview process, I interviewed a lot of siblings who felt left behind after the death of their sibling. If we have the support system in place, we can help them feel more valued and loved. Since I was in the middle of my research and the topic was fresh on my mind, I closely followed social media posts about the holiday season by grieving parents and their children. Social media can trigger sadness around the holidays as grieving parents may be overwhelmed by a stream of family photographs and images of happiness posted by all of their friends. Holiday songs may now bring sadness instead of cheer. Imagine how "I'll Be Home for Christmas" impacts a family whose child will never come home again.

One mother I interviewed told me that Christmas was her child's absolute favorite holiday, and she didn't see how she could ever celebrate Christmas again, even for the sake of the other children. This broke my heart, and made me think about some ways we can really help our loved ones who are hurting during the holiday season.

If a family is skipping out on celebrating events with their children, it could be because it is too painful or it could be because they are simply too overwhelmed to go through the steps to make it happen. Grief is an energy-sucker. But more importantly, significant trauma and grief of this nature often lead to depression. Depression makes it difficult to carry out even simple tasks. And there is nothing simple about the holiday season. Therefore, you might find yourself in a position to bring some happiness to the family and relieve the parents of the burden of having to do it themselves. Do it for the sake of the children. Children will not be able to understand why their parents are not celebrating Christmas with them, why they didn't get a tree or make cookies like they normally do, or why Santa does not show up that year. It may be difficult to believe that grief can shut a family down to this extreme, but it happens.

I spent a lot of time speaking with the children of families who lost a sibling about their experiences over the holiday season. As you might imagine, these children were deeply impacted when their parents were not able to give them the attention they needed during the holidays.

The following suggestions are based on their feedback. As with all suggestions in the book, implement with love and always follow the wishes of the family if they are uncomfortable.

- *Check in on the family around the holidays and offer help and support.*

- *Ask how their holiday planning is coming along and if they have a tree yet or if they have plans.*

- *If it looks like they are not doing anything for the holidays, you can gently express concerns about the children not having a holiday and ask if you can help.*

While it is important that the surviving children are not forgotten and are still getting to experience the joys of the holidays or birthdays, it ultimately is up to the family what they do and how you can help. Going above and beyond their wishes may be traumatic.

Things you can offer:

- *Take the kids shopping to get presents for their parents and siblings*

- *Take the kids out to get a tree*

- *Help decorate the house and tree*

What Do I Do?

- *Make holiday cookies with or for the kids*

- *Go shopping for presents for the kids*

- *Bring cookies over and spend some time with your friend, listening. You should invite them to talk about their deceased child.*

The parents may be too overcome with grief to think of these things the first year or so, but keeping the spirit and memory-making alive is very important for the surviving child or children. If the parents seem overwhelmed by the task of going to buy a tree and gifts, volunteer to take this on for them, as it might just be too painful and too draining for them to do this. However, if they are adamant that they do not want to do a big holiday, their wishes should be respected. Consider purchasing small gifts for the family and deliver those.

OTHER SPECIAL EVENTS

Celebrating birthdays and other childhood milestones can be overwhelming even when you're not grieving. You can help organize one of the children's birthday parties by hosting the party in your own home, or finding a place to gather friends, so the parents don't have to.

RESOURCES FOR TALKING WITH
CHILDREN ABOUT DEATH

https://clinicalcenter.nih.gov/ccc/patient_education/pepubs/childdeath.pdf

https://childdevelopmentinfo.com/how-to-be-a-parent/communication/talk-to-kids-death/

https://www.psychologytoday.com/us/blog/two-takes-depression/201612/the-dos-and-donts-talking-child-about-death

https://www.fredrogers.org/parents/special-challenges/death.php

https://www.parents.com/toddlers-preschoolers/development/social/talking-to-kids-about-death/

Remember, siblings need our **love and support as much as the parents do.**

RETURNING TO SCHOOL

*Death isn't contagious, but sometimes
children think it is.*

Going back to school can be scary and even traumatic to the surviving siblings. Children can have very different feelings about death and if not prepared well for the return of their grieving classmate, can often do and say things that will ostracize and harm the child.

I interviewed countless teachers and guidance counselors for this book. Many of them have not received training or guidance on how to help a grieving child upon their return to school, nor do they really know how to help the other children prepare for the return of the student. We did a lot of research and discussing about the types of things that would be helpful, from the point of the view of the family, the teacher, the other students, and the other school staff. This chapter includes all of those suggestions for all involved in helping the child adjust back into a normal school routine and a list of some resources that can help you learn more about this topic and help teachers and other school staff.

THE OTHER KIDS AT SCHOOL

I had a close friend who lost her brother while she was in middle school. When she went back to school, the other kids wouldn't talk to her. A few days went by, and one of the kids told her they were afraid to talk to her because they might die if they spoke to her. All the kids got together and decided it wasn't safe to talk with her anymore.

This is not an uncommon occurrence. Younger students may be afraid that death is contagious, and one of the best things the school can do in preparation for a child returning to school is to ensure the students understand this is not the case.

As friends of the parents, with permission from the family, you can help by informing the school staff of the situation. If possible, schedule a meeting with any staff in contact with the child—the counselors, the principal, the lunchroom teachers, the bus drivers - to make sure that they're all aware of what has happened. This way, when the siblings come back to school, they feel welcome. It is important to acknowledge the loss once they have returned to school, especially for older kids. If no one says anything to them, they may feel as though no one cares.

The child will probably meet with the school counselor, who is trained in communicating with children after trauma. To alleviate teasing or situations in which kids are scared to talk to the child, you might ask the school counselor if they have any protocol developed for talking about this with the other students prior to the child's return.

If this is not something the school has dealt with before, some resources to consider include the Coalition to Support Grieving Children and the National Alliance of Grieving Children. The Coalition to Support Grieving Students provides presentations and other materials to help counselors educate teachers and staff.

Depending on the school district and policies, the school may need to send something home to parents to alert them of the impending conversation about death.

Some parents are very protective of how to broach this subject and may need forewarning.

COMMUNICATION WITH THE TEACHERS AND SCHOOL STAFF

It's a good idea to have an open line of communication with the school when the child returns. The student may be afraid to leave their parents, who are likely distraught and no longer the parents they once were. They might have their own fears about death, or be worried about how the other children at school are going to respond to them. The parents may appreciate having someone available to drive the children to and from school. This will need to be coordinated with teachers, carpool participants, or anyone else who may be impacted by the change in school transportation. If the child rides the bus, talk to them about making sure they have a bus buddy.

You'll want to know if there are any changes in behaviors, problems with students, or signs that the child is not coping well with their grief. It's not guaranteed that the teacher will have received any kind of training in responding to a grieving child, but you can ask the teacher specifically to keep an eye out for certain behaviors, allow them time to go to the counselor as often as they need it, and make sure the child has a buddy so that they aren't alone. It's important that the child feels safe and always has a friend.

PREPARING THE OTHER STUDENTS

As a teacher or guidance counselor, you may receive many questions and different levels of response to the news of the death of a sibling of a student or the death of a child in the class. In order to be able to answer those questions and help your students cope with the news and the situation, the suggestion is to have younger students write down their thoughts about death. What do they think it means? What questions do they have? What fears? Understanding the baseline of their thoughts and beliefs about death will provide a better starting place from which the teacher and school staff can talk to the children, answer questions, and quell some of the fears.

In many school, the responsibility of supporting their students and helping them understand the situation is left up to the teacher. If the school counselors have been trained, they can help the teachers by educating children on what to do when the surviving sibling returns to class. They will know the right protocol to ensure the students understand what they need to understand and provide an opportunity for the classmates to express their feelings and ask questions.

What Do I Do?

The teacher and counselor can better prepare the students by reminding classmates of the student's loss and how the returning sibling may be different. The student may even cry or be very upset and may lash out at other children, which is a normal part of the grieving process. Children ages four to five tend to act more aggressively when they are hurting. Depending on the age, the child may also tell people that his/her sibling died, talk about death, heaven, the funeral, or other parts of the story.

The classmates can be prepared to understand the surviving sibling is experiencing a variety of emotions that may make them act like a different child than before. Re-acclimating to the classroom can be a lot easier if the other students understand what happened and are equipped with tools that can help them to be a kind friend. The entire world of the sibling has been turned upside down, and the more the teacher and class can prepare to support him or her, the better. The teacher can emphasize to the other students how being friendly, understanding, and patient will make a big difference. It may be scary if the returning child acts out in anger or sadness, but is part of the grieving process.

The children may have many questions about death and loss, so the teacher and counselor should plan to spend time answering these questions. It's better to answer them before the child comes back than have the classmates ask the returning student all of the questions. The discussion may make some children sad or scared. If there are children that are really struggling, consider sending them to the counselors office for more help.

In addition to answering questions and preparing the children for what to say, how to behave is also important. Encourage the classmates to play and have fun and try to get the child laughing. The home environment is likely still a very sad place and the more that can be done to help the child release and have fun, the better. But this is often something they feel like they need permission to do, so encouraging the other children to let them know they want them to play is usually a good thing.

WHAT TO SAY TO THE CHILD

Just as friends and family are concerned about saying the right thing to the children, the school staff also has those concerns. The Coalition of Grieving Children has a great downloadable resource with things not to say and what you should say instead, to help teachers and staff choose the most helpful statements. These can be found in the resources section at the end of the chapter.

Word choices are important when talking about death to children. Younger children tend to take words we say literally, so be careful about telling them things like the baby "went to sleep," "went away," or even the word "lost" can be confusing. In the literal mind of a child, if the sibling is "lost" there's a possibility they'll come home again.

WHAT CAN OTHER CHILDREN SAY?

Along with his own support from the school counselor and teacher, it would be great to show the other students how to best support him. The school counselor and the teacher may provide some examples of things to say and how to act, all based on the child's age. The can offer ways to start a conversation and phrases for the children to say so that they are not afraid to open up a conversation with the child. Allow the children to share their emotions and ensure they are aware it is okay to be emotional.

Try not to put limitations on what the children can or can't understand, especially without having a conversation with them to gauge what they do and do not know. Even young children (over the age of 3 or 4) can understand sadness and will often want to hug or console their friend. Children over the age of five understand that death is final, even if they don't have a full grasp on the situation. Try to remind them not to ask a lot of questions when the sibling returns to school, and offer them the time and safe space to ask those questions to the teacher or counselor.

For older children, you can start to teach them maybe a few things to say, like, "I'm sorry." If they knew the sibling, they can say nice things and share their memories about them. Encourage them to give permission to their grieving friend to talk about the sibling and share their feelings. Students need to know it's okay not to have all the answers, and that it's okay to just listen. If they are concerned about anything their friend shares with them, they should inform the teacher or counselor. Concerning statements could include a desire to hurt themselves, feeling as if they have no purpose in life anymore, or placing blame on themselves for their sibling's death.

FOR THE TEACHER & CLASS OF THE STUDENT WHO DIED

Children will obviously notice when a child does not return to school. They will have many questions. What happened? Where did they go? Are they coming back? Did they do something wrong? Talking to the children, answering their questions, and providing a safe space, time, and a place for them to access the school counselor if they are feeling upset are some of the best solutions to avoid confusion and fear.

Helping children cope with the loss of a sibling or class-mate and providing healthy opportunities for expressing their emotions will be a very important part of their healing and emotional development.

"Each year I prepare my daughter's teachers that my daughter may tell them about her sister that died. She wants to make sure everyone remembers her. And I want the teachers to know this is not abnormal or weird, but a part of her coping process."
~Marie's mom

SOME RESOURCES FOR THE SCHOOL FOR TALKING WITH CHILDREN ABOUT DEATH

School Crisis Center
https://www.schoolcrisiscenter.org/projects/coalition-to-support-grieving-students/

Grieving Students
http://grievingstudents.org/wp-content/uploads/2016/05/NYL-1B-What-to-Say.pdf
http://grievingstudents.org/wp-content/uploads/2016/05/NYL-1D-Peer-Support.pdf

National Association of School Psychologists (NASP)
https://www.nasponline.org/resources-and-publications/resources-and-podcasts/school-climate-safety-and-crisis/mental-health-resources/addressing-grief/addressing-grief-tips-for-teachers-and-administrators

National Institutes of Health
https://clinicalcenter.nih.gov/ccc/patient_education/pepubs/childdeath.pdf

Psychology Today

https://www.psychologytoday.com/us/blog/
two-takes-depression/201612/the-dos-and-donts-talking-
child-about-death

Other resources are widely available at the library and online.

RETURNING TO WORK

I felt alone and full of despair as all of my co-workers ignored me or talked about me behind my back.

Returning to work can be a blessing for some people who desperately need the distraction, and a nightmare for others who are experiencing anxiety, overwhelming grief, and are in what many parents will later describe as a "fog." It may be difficult to concentrate and complete even basic tasks for some people. The parent may be distracted, easily agitated, or easily saddened. Some people are able to compartmentalize and throw themselves back into work while others will really struggle to make it through the day.

One mother shared that although it had been almost a year since her son passed away, she still found it difficult to concentrate on work and really even care anymore about the tasks she was expected to complete. She also mentioned that she felt nervous about saying anything to her co-workers because she got the vibe from them that they expected her to be "over it" by now and functioning in the workplace. Those co-workers who have never been through a situation like this may only be sympathetic to a certain extent. Then they expect the employee to get back to work, move on, and be productive.

During this time, as a friend and support network, you can really make a difference by letting your friend know you are thinking about them. Check in regularly to see how your friend is doing. If it seems as though they are struggling (or even if they aren't outwardly struggling) you can help lighten the load.

Some tasks you can assume:

- *Taking the children to school or picking them up*

- *Taking the children to afterschool activities*

- *Call your friend, text, or email each day to make sure they are doing okay*

- *Take your friend to lunch to get them out of the office*

- *Visit in the evenings*

- *Make sure there are meals arriving*

- *Help with grocery shopping and errands*

If you know any of their co-workers well, or if a co-worker has reached out to see how they can be helpful, you might also share some tips with them on making the office environment easier for the parent.

MY STORY

Every story is different but one thing is the same across all of them. The person, regardless of how well they look like they are functioning on the outside may actually be moments away from completely losing it.

My situation is definitely different from many other parents. I actually got fired on the same day my six-month-old baby girl died. I had been a nanny for twenty years and suddenly I was unemployed and absolutely reeling from the loss of child. I had no idea what to do or where to go. In order to help me get back on track and pull myself together again, someone in my inner circle suggested I find a job immediately. So, I put out some feelers and a friend of mine was kind enough to help me find a job.

Only six days after Paris died, I returned to work. A new job, with new people I did not know. I hoped that I'd be able to start from scratch and slide in under the radar. But my friend, who thought he was being helpful, let everyone know my situation before I arrived. Instead of just being the new girl, I was now the new girl who had just suffered a major tragedy, and people were afraid of talking to me.

When I walked into the office, everyone was whispering and no one would look at me or speak with me. I was an outcast. I would go to the bathroom and just cry—I had no one—no support whatsoever. It was as if "Yes, I lost my daughter" flashed like a neon light from my forehead. I had the one friend who would invite me to lunch and check up on me, but no one else would include me in anything.

I was riddled with anxiety and completely alone. I kept to myself and focused on the tasks I had to get done so that I could survive the work day. Then each evening I returned to my home and just cried.

I had no support at home, because another part of my tragedy included the end of my marriage in this same timeframe. My parents were not in town or able to come help me. I was alone and I was really struggling. The people I needed to be there were not there in the way I needed them to be. I knew immediately that going back to work so soon was a bad idea.

I asked my boss for a week off. Rather than showing any compassion to my situation, my boss said no, because I had just started the job and he considered me necessary. I often wondered why bosses in this situation realize that a person who is reeling from a trauma of this nature is not usually a good asset at work either.

I became depressed and had thoughts of hurting myself. I felt like I had two choices at this point. I could either kill myself and join my daughter in the afterlife, or I needed to make a big change and get away from this place. I lasted about one month or so in this horrible environment before I decided to move away. Essentially, to save and protect myself from becoming further depressed, I left my job, my home, everything, and moved to Florida, vowing I would start a new life and never talk about the death of my daughter again.

While the circumstances of my situation are unique to me, the bigger picture is that your friend and/or co-worker may really be dealing with a lot of issues both at home and at work. How you decide to respond and handle this situation is really important. If anyone had made any efforts to reach out, speak to me, and try to make me feel more comfortable in that environment, it could have made a huge difference.

HOW TO HELP YOUR CO-WORKER

In many organizations, bereavement policies are in place for only four days, while some states have enacted policies for up to 10 working days after the death of a child. Four days is not going to be enough time for most people to function again in the workplace. The parent may be distracted, uncomfortable, emotional, and unable to focus on any major task.

MANAGERS AND ADMINISTRATION

Managers and administration have a responsibility to help the person transition back into work. Coordinate a team meeting to speak with the other co-workers to give some suggestions on how to respond when the grieving parent returns to work.

- Be flexible and forgiving.
- Show compassion.
- Have realistic expectations.
- And if they need extra time, allow them to take it.

Returning to Work

As a co-worker, there are things that you can do to soften the return to work, such as greeting them with a warm hug, or if you aren't that close with the grieving co-worker, leaving a card on their desk, or flowers or something to let them know you are sad for them. Take the time to actually speak to them and acknowledge their situation. Try being mindful to let them know you are thinking of them. You can do this by offering a listening ear.

Some ideas on things to say:

- *"I'm sorry."*

- *"You're in my thoughts and prayers."*

- *"I'm always available to listen."*

Acknowledging the child is important. Most parents never want their child to be forgotten. It might be difficult to bring the child up in conversation if you were not friends with this person prior to their loss. If you feel comfortable doing so, you may embrace your colleague in a big hug. Placing your hand on their arm in support may also be comforting, depending on your relationship. Just as the siblings needed a buddy system when they returned to school, the parent may also need a safe person at work.

What Do I Do?

Here are some ideas on how to be supportive:

- *Invite the friend to go out to lunch or take a coffee break.*

- *Stop by their office to talk.*

- *If there is a picture of the child on their desk, be prepared to say something about the child. If you didn't know their child, you could admire the photo and mention how much the child looked like them, or simply mention what a great photo it is.*

- *Perhaps avoid talking about your children in the first few days, especially if the child who died was an only child.*

- *Ask about the other children.*

- *See if there is any way you can be of help. The person may not have a family support system, and co-workers may want to volunteer to help them with meals and other tasks.*

It may become obvious that they are really struggling. Some simple suggestions to help in this case are:

- *Encourage the parent to breathe*
- *Provide assistance with overwhelming tasks in the office place*
- *Create a "return to work survival kit" that includes items*

such as stress relief lotion, essential oils, tissues, a rock with the child's name on it, chocolate, tea, and other items

*"Grieving the loss of a child
starts the day
we lose our child,
and ends the day
we join them."*
~ Unknown

SUPPORT FOR MEN

Grief is like living two lives.

Men and women respond to the death of a child differently. They also grieve differently. Men are hurting just as much as women are and they need the same support as women do, even if this does not seem obvious by their actions.

Some men may take longer to heal because stereotypically, men do not talk about their emotions openly, and tend to appear as if they have moved on more quickly. In many cultures, men are raised to be less emotional and the head of the family, perhaps making them believe they have to be the strong one. Because of this stigma against showing their grief, they don't always allow themselves to deal with the death in the beginning, and may even push it to the back of their minds. While trying to be strong for their family, they are suffering. At some point, it may catch up to them, but others will compartmentalize these feelings forever.

Just because men tell you they're okay, doesn't mean they are. If you are the friend of a grieving father, you can make a weekly plan with them as well, to check in regularly for the first few months. Give them a safe space to vent and share their emotions. They may feel exhausted from being strong for their partner and need an outlet.

The inability to grieve out loud can result in a longer healing time for fathers. As with any other person, the unresolved grief will eventually catch up with them. Sometimes this manifests in troubles within the marriage, anger, or acting out in other ways, disconnecting, or spending time alone. Find some ways to get him out to do some things he enjoys and allow him an ear. It's also important to let this man know that it's okay to cry, and you will not judge him for shedding tears.

Initially, you might not get any interest the first few times you invite the dad out. Keep trying. He may be hurting too badly to go out into the world, or he may be afraid to leave his spouse alone. If you can try to invite him somewhere when you know his partner is also occupied, that may help him feel more at ease about leaving. You don't have to make a big deal about his emotions, because some men will continue to just tell you that they're "okay." Remain strong. Protect the family. Find some way to connect and provide opportunities for them to share.

Just make sure that you don't give up, even if they continue to make excuses. Invite them to do something you know they enjoy doing—going to a sporting event, a concert or invite them to train for a 5K. Eventually, they will take you up on your invitation. Call, text, drop by, offer to help them with an ongoing project. Ask them to help you with a project at your home. Sometimes that's easier because they think they are helping you.

I had a conversation with a dear male friend of mine, Peter Anthony Wynne, who lost his daughter. The following passage is his advice for supporting a father after a child dies. This is his perspective and may not speak to how all men will respond or feel about these issues, but it is a good insight into how some men grieve, heal, and need to be supported after their child dies.

What Do I Do?

A 12-MONTH PLAN TO SUPPORT A FAMILY WHOSE CHILD DIED—A FATHER'S PERSPECTIVE

BY PETER ANTHONY WYNN

First:

The best way you can help a man who is grieving the loss of his child is to take on the burden of caring for the wife and children emotionally and physically. Men are often completely stressed and don't make the time to rest emotionally because they are trying to be strong.

Advice is not helpful, (advice may make the father question whether he could have done something differently, whether he was a good enough father, etc which is not good for mental health) but listening and understanding are two of the best things you can do.

Alone time is critical. Reinforcement is also crucial. Meaning, saying encouraging things like: "you're doing a great job, stay strong, the children love and need you." These simple, encouraging statements reinforce what they should be thinking about, which is their family and their home, their job and their role in the family.

You can help reassure his family by reminding them when we lose a child we "feel" like we are the ones who need to hold on to everyone, it is our nature. If he is short-tempered or removed, remind the family how much they are loved by him and how much they mean to him even if they are not feeling it or seeing it.

Initially:

KEEP AWAY: keep away from pictures and reminders, this is important throughout the support process, your support must be thought out.

Never ask how it happened, ever—ever! This is really the worst thing you could ever do to the loved one of anyone, especially a parent.

First Four Months:

Distract with simple things, like the gym, hike, bike ride, or walk. The best thing to do is ask for help with simple things (and make them real or he will see through it), but he needs to get his confidence back and helping friends and family do things that are simple but require him are important. Yard work, painting, cleaning the garage, moving furniture—simple things that require more than one person.

Four to Eight Months:

Redirect pain; this is where you may introduce simple,

new skills to work within the neuroplasticity of the brain and start to create new pathways.

Eight to Twelve Months and Beyond:

Safe space: I am not sure where I am, even in my own life. Two-and-a-half years after losing my sweet baby girl, it still hurts in my heart while writing this.

You never know when the loss and finality will hit. Teaching us where to grieve is key for most men; they need to do this in privacy, it is not a group coaching game. They need to find a way back, they need to know it is ok.

For the Grieving Family:

Men and women heal differently, as do children, and we all look for ways to help when we lose those we raise. My belief is that the greatest way to help is to live, do the things you were born to do!

Create new happy memories. Take your child's spirit with you on your adventure.

Toast to them on the peak of the mountain you want to climb, not the one they wanted to climb. Embrace that time is short and we all must live fully with the time we are given.

When children die, we have a tendency to see what they could have been... where their journey may have taken them. My belief is that when their journey is over, the journey was only designed to inspire your aspiration. The journey of the child is not intended to steal what life is left from those they loved by replacing their loved one's "dreams and desires" with the lost soul's journey. Their journey has ended and it cannot be replaced, it can only fuel your dreams and fill your heart and strengthen your resolve.

RESOURCES FOR GRIEVING FATHERS

Grieving Dads

https://grievingdads.com/

The Good Grief Trust

The Difference Between Grieving Mothers and Fathers
- https://www.thegoodgrieftrust.org/child/couples-and-grief/

Love to Know

https://dying.lovetoknow.com/Grieving_the_Loss_of_a_Child

*"...No mother loses a child without believing she failed as a parent. **No father loses a child without believing he failed to protect his family from pain.** The child may be gone, but the years the child were meant to live remain behind, solid in the mind like an aging ghost. The birthdays, the holidays, the last days of school—they all remain, circled in red lipstick on a calendar nailed to the wall. A constant shadow that grows, even in the dark. As I was saying...there are no words."*
~D.E. Eliot, Ruined

FUTURE DAYS

*Just because we have a good day,
do not assume we are okay.*

The path to healing can be a long one; one that takes strength, courage, and sometimes comes down to just taking one step after another, baby steps to survival. It requires time and a commitment to making a choice each day to move forward and live again.

The point of this book was to show you that friends and family who are engaged with the grieving family will make the transition into finding a routine within their "new normal" and find the path to healing easier. As a friend, you play a key role in easing the grieving parents back into life.

The cycle of grief can be confusing. While you may witness your friend moving from one stage to another, sometimes a triggering event can pop them right back into sadness, anger, or disbelief. Some days they may be happy and full of joy, and the next day, a simple word or sound may throw them back to a state of sadness. All of these are normal.

As part of their support system, it's important to take each day one at a time and know this is a lifelong journey filled with ups and downs. So please never give up on the grieving parents and understand that they will never be the same person they were before. Eventually, when they least expect it, it won't hurt as much, and you will have contributed to that magic moment. After everyone has moved on with their daily lives, your love and support will make a difference in their healing and their path forward.

"*I wonder if I would still be so angry and struggling so hard after five years if my friends and family had been there more for me in the first year after we lost our daughter? I think they would have really made a difference in who I became.*"
~ Carla

APPENDIX A: FOR THE GRIEVING PARENT

YOUR STORY AS THE GRIEVING PARENT: COPING WITH THE GRIEF

I wrote this book for the people who are supporting the family after a child dies, but I know there will be many grieving parents who decide to pick up this book and share it with their networks. So this section is a message especially for you.

We each have a unique story surrounding our loss, but the one thing that is not unique is the need to cope with the grief. We rely on our friends and family to be there for us and have certain expectations that when we need them, they will do all things possible to ease our pain. But knowing what to do does not come easily to most people.

As I shared in the introduction of the book, my daughter died of SIDS in 2003. My world crumbled to pieces. At a time when I needed support from those around me more than anything, I had very little. Perhaps my friends believed my parents would take care of me, but honestly, my mother was also also grieving the loss of her granddaughter.

It's not that your friends and family don't want to help you, they are just often paralyzed in this situation. Our friends and family need a resource guide to show them how to help. So that we don't wind up alone and depressed and contemplating hurting ourselves.

Everyone's life went back to normal and I was left to fend for myself. I tried to move on by jumping back into work, but that was a terrible experience and I came home every day and cried. I became so depressed and decided I had two choices; either I would commit suicide to be with my daughter, or, I was going to completely abandon my life and start new somewhere else. Thankfully, I chose option B.

At the time, my parents were off living their dream, sailing the world. This offered an opportunity for me to escape because they had a beautiful condo in Florida that was vacant, overlooking the gulf. I was able to live in this beautiful world, looking at the ocean as I drank my coffee, leaving behind my troubles and sorrows.

Life was better. Shortly before I left my old life, I met the man I am married to now, and we fell in love. He came with me to Florida, and we started our life together. I thought I had successfully run away from that painful period. I began to dream about having more children.

Happiness would not come easily for me. Tragedy struck again and I had three miscarriages over the next year. We had testing done and I was told there was nothing wrong with me physically, but I was probably too stressed, causing my body to miscarry. My husband took a job in Tulsa, Oklahoma, and we moved to a place where life was slow, calm, and I could focus on being healthy.

Finally, I became pregnant with my first son, who was also born with extreme complications and we nearly lost him. Thankfully, he survived and was healthy. Then I had a second son a couple years later. I committed myself to raising the boys, homeschooling them, and traveling. Life was good, but somewhere during this timeframe I found myself unexpectedly sucker punched with another wave of grief and depression.

There are a lot of moving pieces to my story, but an important piece of how I got to where I am now begins with Loren. I had met and become friends with a coach,

Loren Lahav. Loren was running women's retreats, and I decided to attend one. When I showed up I wasn't sure what I wanted to gain from the event. I just knew I was depressed, suffering, and wanted more from life.

At this event, I met Jennifer Steinman Sternin, the producer of the movie "Motherhood." This film is all about parents who lost children. As soon as she started talking, I lost all composure, crying. I realized my depression stemmed from the grief I buried years ago when Paris died. Loren helped me brainstorm ways I could work through this grief, build myself up again, and find a way to make a positive impact on the world through my personal journey.

Now that I knew my path forward, I wanted to connect to as many other grieving parents as possible. I needed to find out if they'd had a similar experience I joined some support groups for grieving parents and I started interviewing them. I spent thousands of hours discussing their stories, and we came to realize that the common thread for all of us was that we needed more help from our friends and family after our child died. Loren encouraged me to write a book, which I thought was a crazy idea at first. But eventually, I realized that it was bigger than just about me. It was about helping others, potentially even saving lives if I was able to offer advice and support that could help another parent from getting to the state of suicidal depression like I had been.

Appendix A: For the Grieving Parent

I knew if I could help other people learn how to deal with other people's grief, I could make a big impact on the world.

You also must find a way to face your grief and begin the process of healing. Your journal may not look just like mine, but I encourage you to find a way to start. I thought I could run away from the pain of the loss, start my life over and move on. But that unresolved grief caught up with me, in so many ways. Whether the grief is fresh and new, or some amount of time has passed, you will have to confront it eventually. It may not come back for a long time, but eventually, unresolved grief will manifest itself in other areas of your life.

If you find yourself without a support network, or you're not comfortable speaking to a friend or family member, finding a local therapist, or visiting a religious leader or local support group, consider finding some online support networks.

There are many online support groups and places where grieving parents can connect with other parents who understand them and "get it." I've listed many resources in the following section, as a starting place.

You are always welcome to reach out to me as well.

GRIEF RESOURCES

This resource section is not meant to be in place of your support as friends and family. Rather, this is a list of additional tools and resources to help you if you're looking for more ways to help, more places to find suggestions, or if you're the grieving parent and you want to find other groups and resources as you begin your healing journey.

There are many, many resources for grieving parents, whether you are looking for books or blogs to read, tokens of remembrance, or communities. The following is a list of some of our favorite sites and resources. It is certainly not inclusive.

Grief Resources

BOOKS

If you are seeking further help and support as a grieving parent, these are just some of the many books available.

Sunshine After the Storm: A Survival Guide for the Grieving Mother edited by Alexa Bigwarfe

Empty Arms by Sherokee Ilse

You Are the Mother of All Mothers by Angie Miller

Three Minus One: Parents' Stories of Love & Loss Edited by Sean Hanish and Brooke Warner

Grieving Dads: To the Brink and Back by Kelly Farley

I Will Carry You: The Sacred Dance of Grief and Joy by Angie Smith

Navigating the Unknown by Amie Lands

What Do I Do?

The Other "F" Word: When Faith Fills the Gap by Sara Stamp

Surviving My First Year of Child Loss: Personal Stories From Grieving Parents by Nathalie Himmelrich

Grief Resources

WEBSITES

These are just a few of the amazing support networks available. If none of these is a good fit for you, an internet search will return in hundreds of results.

A
A Bed for My Heart
https://abedformyheart.com/

A Place to Remember (bookstore, gift items)
http://www.aplacetoremember.com/

B
Babies Remembered:
http://www.BabiesRemembered.org

Baby Angel Pics (photo retouching)
http://www.babyangelpics.com/

Bereaved Parents of the USA
http://www.bereavedparentsusa.org/

Bereavement Store
http://bereavementstore.com/

C

Casting Keepsakes
http://www.castingkeepsakes.com/

Christian's Beach (names written in the sand)
http://namesinthesand.blogspot.com/

CLIMB (Center for Loss in Multiple Births)
http://www.climb-support.org/

Compassionate Friends (support for loss)
http://www.compassionatefriends.org/home.aspx

F

Faces of Loss Faces of Hope (local support)
http://facesofloss.com/

G

Grief Song (grief songs)
http://www.griefsong.com/

Grieving Parents Network
https://grievingparents.net/

H

Halo Garden
http://www.halogarden.com/

Hannah's Prayer
http://www.hannah.org

Healing Hearts (information)
http://www.babylosscomfort.com/grief-resources/

Heartbreaking Choice (For parents who have terminated
due to poor prenatal diagnosis)
http://www.aheartbreakingchoice.com/

I

In the Face of Loss (on making time and space for grief)
http://Www.inthefaceofloss.com

In the Name of the Fire (grief website)
http://inthenameofthefire.wordpress.com/

L

Little Angels Online Store

http://www.littleangelsonlinestore.com/Store/

Living with Loss Magazine
http://www.livingwithloss.com/page.cfm?pageid=9009

Loss Doulas International
http://www.LossDoulasInternational.com

M
Memory Of (memorial website)
http://www.memory-of.com/Public/

MEND
http://www.mend.orgMikayla's Grace (provides care packages to grieving parents, WI)
http://www.mikaylasgrace.com

Molly Bears (bear created in the same weight as your baby)
http://www.mollybears.com/

Mommies with Hope
http://www.mommieswithhope.com

My Forever Child (keepsakes and jewelry)
http://www.myforeverchild.com/

N

Nechamama Comfort (Jewish pregnancy and loss support program)
http://www.nechamacomfort.org

Now I Lay Me Down To Sleep (photography)
http://www.nowilaymedowntosleep.org/

No Holding Back (blog on life after loss)
http://katbiggie.com

O

October 15th (pregnancy and infant loss awareness)
http://www.october15th.com/

P

Perfect Joy Ministries
http://www.perfectjoyministries.com

Pencil Portraits by Dana
http://portraitsbydana.com/

Piggie Paws (creates handprints/footprints into something else) http://www.piggiesandpaws.com/

Project Heal (and International Bereaved Mother's Day)
http://carlymarieprojectheal.com/

R
Rainbows and Redemption: Encouragement for the
Journey of Pregnancy After Loss
http://www.rainbowsandredemption.weebly.com

Remembering Our Babies (memorial keepsakes and
jewelry)
http://www.rememberingourbabies.net/

Return to Zero
http://returntozerothemovie.com/

S
SHARE (pregnancy/infant loss support groups)
http://www.nationalshare.org/

SPALS (pregnancy after loss)
http://www.spals.com/home/index.html

Stillborn and Still Breathing
http://www.stillbornandstillbreathing.com

Stillborn Memorial (pencil sketches)

http://www.stillbornmemorial.com

Still Standing Magazine
http://stillstandingmag.com

Sufficient Grace Ministries
http://www.sufficientgraceministries.org

Sunshine After the Storm
http://sunshineafterstorm.us/

T
Teeny Tears
http://www.teenytears.blogspot.com

The Greatest Blessing (memory boxes)
http://www.greatestblessing.blogspot.com/

V
Virtual Memorials (create remembrance site)
http://www.virtual-memorials.com/

ACKNOWLEDGMENTS

Thank you to my husband, Jim Calabrese, for all of his love and support and allowing me to follow my dreams. You are my rock and best friend.

Thank you, Heather Sandberg, for being the first person to arrive at the hospital and never leaving my side.

Also, a special thank you to Julie Beller Lingenfelter for never leaving my side during the worst days of my life.

What Do I Do?

*Thank you to every single family member
and friend who stayed with me during
the most horrific days of my life.*

*And finally, thank you Loren Lahav, my friend,
coach, and mentor, for believing in me before I believed in myself. You taught me to take the worse
situation of my life and turn it into a way to give
back and help people. I am forever grateful.*

ABOUT THE AUTHOR

Kimberly Calabrese lost her daughter, Paris, when her baby was just six months old. During this incredibly painful time in her life, Kimberly did not have a lot of support because her friends and family felt helpless, not knowing what to do. So, Kimberly chose to pretend it didn't happen, moved to another state, and buried Paris's death deep inside her heart for over ten years.

However, Kimberly discovered the harsh reality that the loss of a child can never be forgotten—no matter how far you run or how busy you are. She has since dedicated herself to healing others who have suffered a tragic loss.

Kimberly lives with her husband, James, and two sons, Chance and Blayne in Connecticut. Second only to helping others, her passion is travel. Kimberly homeschools her two boys and teaches them through travel. Kimberly has been to China, Thailand, and all through Europe with her family.

Kimberly is available for speaking, consulting and radio interviews.

You can reach her at:

Kimberly@SupportOfALovedOne.com